AIRCRAFT

Julie Dos Santos

This edition first published in 2010 in the United States of America by Marshall Cavendish Benchmark.

Marshall Cavendish Benchmark
99 White Plains Road
Tarrytown, NY 10591
www.marshallcavendish.us

Library of Congress Cataloging-in-Publication Data

Dos Santos, Julie.
    Aircraft / by Julie Dos Santos.
        p. cm. -- (Amazing machines)
        Summary: "Discusses the different kinds of aircraft, what they are used for, and how they work"--Provided by publisher.
        Includes bibliographical references and index.
        ISBN 978-0-7614-4404-6
1. Airplanes--Juvenile literature. I. Title.
        TL547.D67 2010
        629.13--dc22
        2008054367

The photographs in this book are used by permission and through the courtesy of:
t=top b=bottom c=center l=left r=right m=middle
Cover Photos: Shutterstock; (Inset): Denise Kappa /Shutterstock, Background: Liga Lauzuma/Shutterstock
Title Photo: Aero Graphics, Inc./Corbis
Content Page: Sascha Hahn/Shutterstock; BG: Alon Brik/Shutterstock

4-5: Stephen Strathdee/Shutterstock; 6-7: Sasha Radosavljevic/123rf; 7(inset): Roger Walker/Fotolia; 8-9: dan_prat/iStockphoto; 9(inset): Ivan Hafizov/Fotolia; 10-11BG: Alon Brik/Shutterstock; 10-11: Charles Polidano / Touch The Skies/Alamy; 11(inset): Uwe Bumann/Shutterstock; 12-13BG: Alon Brik/Shutterstock; 12: Ponomaryov Vlad/Shutterstock; 13(inset): DanCardiff/iStockphoto; 14-15BG: Alon Brik/Shutterstock; 14-15: Sascha Hahn/Shutterstock; 15(inset): Aero Graphics, Inc./Corbis; 16-17BG: thumb/Shutterstock; 16-17: Sascha Hahn/Shutterstock; 17(inset): Jathys/Shutterstock; 18-19: Icholakov/Fotolia; 19(inset): Regien Paassen/Shutterstock; 20-21BG: Serg64/Shutterstock; 20-21: Andriy Rovenko/Shutterstock; 21(inset): Michael Koehl/Dreamstime; 22-23: Bobby Deal / RealDealPhoto/Shutterstock; 23(inset): Karl R. Martin/Shutterstock; 24-25:NASA; 25(inset): Alan Freed/Shutterstock; 26(inset): Danny Johnston/Associated Press; 26-27: Wong Chee Yen/Dreamstime; 28-29: Charles Polidano / Touch The Skies / Alamy; 30-31: Deejpilot/iStockphoto; 32BG: Shutterstock.

Art Director: Sumit Charles

Client Service Manager: Santosh Vasudevan

Project Manager: Shekhar Kapur

Editor: Penny Dowdy

Designer: Ritu Chopra

Photo Researcher: Shreya Sharma

Printed in Malaysia
1 3 5 6 4 2

Contents

What Is an Aircraft?

An **aircraft** is a machine that flies. People wanted to fly long before they knew how. Today people can fly in many kinds of machines.

This airplane can take people thousands of miles in a matter of hours.

Airplanes and helicopters allow people to travel far in short amounts of time. Driving across the United States could take days. Flying that far can take just a few hours.

Biplanes

The first powered airplane was a **biplane** built by the Wright brothers. They built their plane, *The Flyer*, in 1903. Biplanes have two long wings, one above the other, that stretch across the plane.

The propeller spins very fast.

A biplane has two wings, one above the other.

The wheels are called the landing gear.

Biplanes are still used today in air shows and for dusting crops.

The struts hold up the wings.

This is called the tailplane or stabilizer.

Biplanes are **fixed-wing** planes. This means the wings do not move. The tail controls whether the plane flies up, down, or straight. Flaps on the wings help the plane turn.

This biplane looks like the one the Wright Brothers built.

Commercial Airplanes

Commercial airplanes take people from place to place. Some are huge. An Airbus can carry more than 800 passengers! People started traveling by airplane in the 1930s.

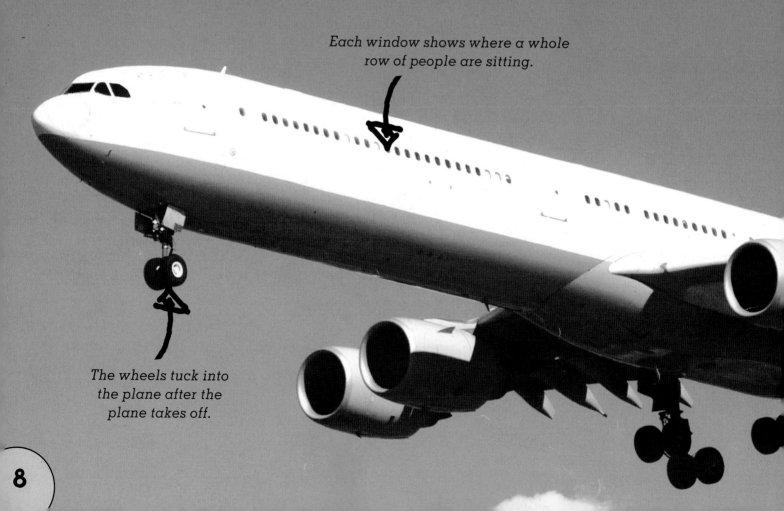

Each window shows where a whole row of people are sitting.

The wheels tuck into the plane after the plane takes off.

Commercial airplanes use jet engines to travel fast. The more fuel they hold, the farther they can fly without stopping. Planes can fly from Asia to North America non-stop!

Seats in the airplane are close together. An aisle down the middle gives space where people can walk.

This plane needs four engines to provide the power needed to fly.

The stabilizer tilts the airplane up and down. It keeps the plane level when it flies straight.

This large Airbus can carry hundreds of people.

Freight Airplanes

Freight airplanes carry packages, not people. They are also called cargo airplanes. These planes are much bigger than commercial airplanes. The packages, or cargo, take up more room than people.

The tail is called the rudder. The flap on the rudder moves the plane left or right.

This plane has big engines to lift the heavy freight off the ground.

The tail of a freight airplane sits above a large door. Trucks can drive through the door and onto the plane with the cargo.

The cargo hold on the freight airplane is huge!

Freight airplanes do not need windows on the side. There are no passengers on the plane.

The pilot and copilot control the plane from the cockpit.

FedEx Express

The World On Time

Helicopters

A **helicopter** flies in a different way than a plane. It has blades on top that whirl around and lift it up. Helicopters need just a flat space to take off and land.

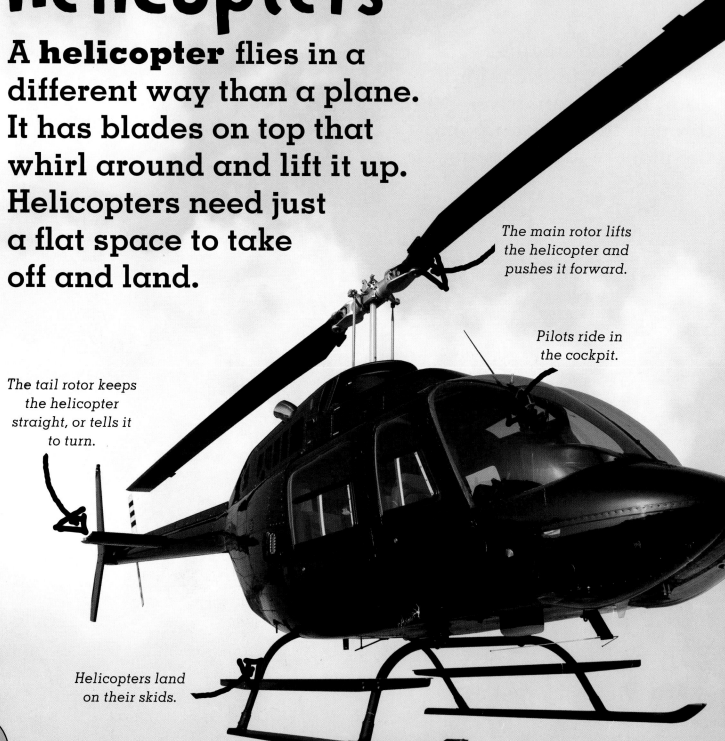

The main rotor lifts the helicopter and pushes it forward.

Pilots ride in the cockpit.

The tail rotor keeps the helicopter straight, or tells it to turn.

Helicopters land on their skids.

This helicopter has wheels
instead of skids.

Some helicopters can carry only a small amount
of cargo. Others can carry a great deal of weight.
Helicopters can **hover**, or stay in one place in the
air. Most airplanes cannot hover.

Military Airplanes

Military airplanes use weapons in battle. Fighting planes do not have room for cargo. They hold very few people. Some planes fly by remote control with no pilot.

The wings hold engines and weapons.

This military jet has room only for the crew and weapons.

The pilot can see all around the plane from the cockpit.

Weapons here protect the plane from attack.

Some military airplanes can spy on enemies from high in the sky. These planes take pictures of enemy soldiers and cities while the plane flies.

This plane is a B2 bomber. The wings and tail have an unusual design.

Osprey

An **Osprey** takes off and lands like a helicopter. Then its propellers tilt, and it flies like an airplane. The Osprey carries either cargo or people.

A small crew rides in the cabin behind the cockpit.

Soldiers ride in the back of the plane until the Osprey takes them where they are needed.

In this picture, the propellers face up. They lift the machine up.

Ospreys fly higher and faster than helicopters. Like helicopters, they do not need a runway. They can work in small spaces. The military uses Ospreys to carry troops and weapons.

A machine gun is attached to the ramp so the osprey is protected from enemies.

In this picture, the propellers face forward. They move the machine forward.

Corporate Jets

Another word for business is *corporate*. A jet used by a business is a **corporate jet**. Businesses own planes so that workers can fly wherever and whenever they want to.

Small jets have rudders and stabilizers, just like big jets.

This corporate jet is just the right size for a few people and their luggage.

Corporate jets carry fewer passengers than commercial airplanes. Sometimes they have desks, chairs, and computers on board. This way the passengers can work while they fly.

Cockpits are usually just big enough for one person.

Not all jets have engines on the wings. Some use propellers.

The pilot uses many controls to fly and land the plane.

Seaplanes

Seaplanes can take off and land on water. Seaplanes can take people to places without airports. All a seaplane needs is a large body of water.

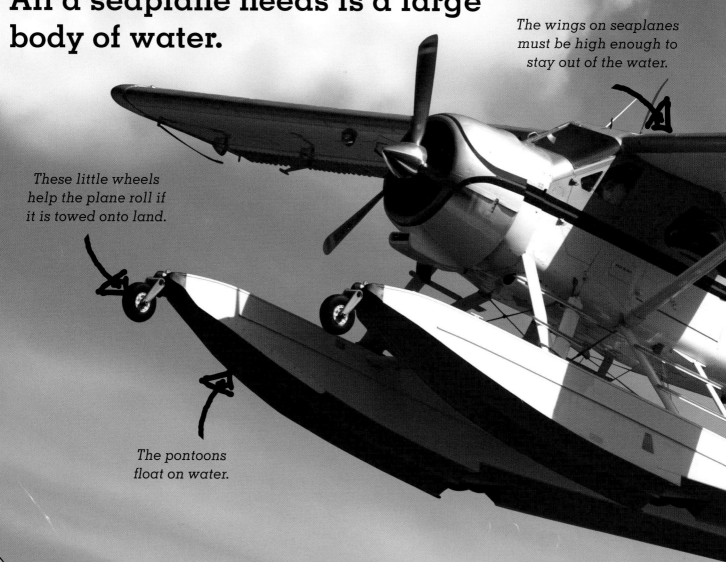

The wings on seaplanes must be high enough to stay out of the water.

These little wheels help the plane roll if it is towed onto land.

The pontoons float on water.

Seaplanes land on water, not the ground.

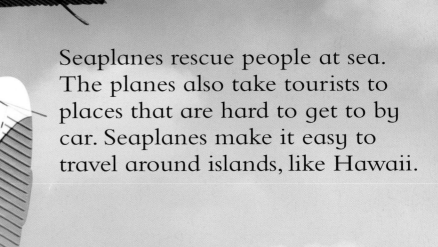

Seaplanes rescue people at sea. The planes also take tourists to places that are hard to get to by car. Seaplanes make it easy to travel around islands, like Hawaii.

Seaplanes can fly people to places with water, but no airport.

Blimps

Blimps fly, but they are not airplanes. They have no wings. Instead, they are huge airships filled with air and **helium**. Helium is the same gas used to fill balloons.

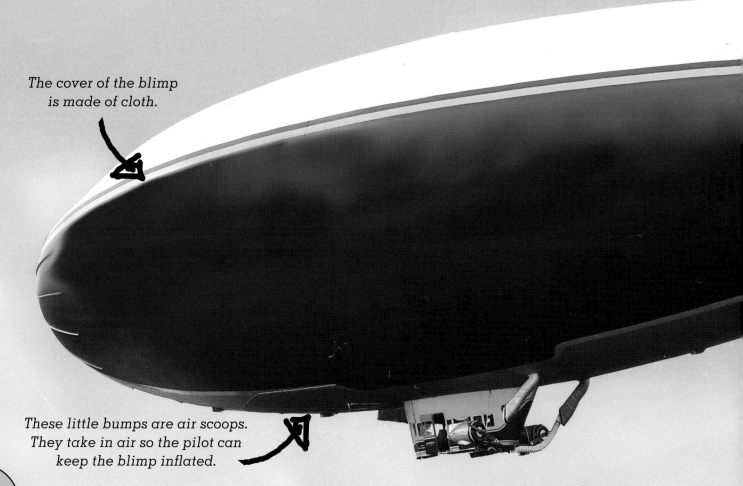

The cover of the blimp is made of cloth.

These little bumps are air scoops. They take in air so the pilot can keep the blimp inflated.

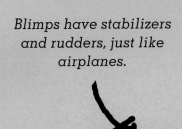

Blimps have stabilizers and rudders, just like airplanes.

The gondola windows let the passengers see the great view.

Cloth covers the blimp on the outside. Inside, two huge bags hold air. The bags take in or let out air. The movement of the air makes the blimp go up and down. Propellers move the blimp forward or backward.

The gas in the blimp lifts it off the ground.

Shuttle Carrier Aircraft

The **Shuttle Carrier Aircraft** carries a space shuttle. A space shuttle cannot take off by itself. A rocket launches the shuttle into space. The aircraft flies the shuttle on Earth.

The struts hold the space shuttle in place.

The Shuttle Carrier Aircraft at first was an ordinary airplane. NASA removed most of the insides. They added stronger engines. This plane carries cargo on the outside instead of inside.

The space shuttle needs rockets to get it to space.

The body of the airplane is called the fuselage.

NASA remodeled an ordinary plane to make it stronger. Now it is strong enough to carry the space shuttle on its back!

Summing Up

Aircraft include planes, helicopters, and blimps. All of these machines help people travel over long distances. They help travelers, businesses, and the military.

The Blue Angels is the name of a team of military aircraft.

Some aircraft use propellers. Others use jet engines or gasses. Since the Wright brothers invented the airplane, flying machines have moved people and packages all over the world.

Amazing Facts

- The biplane *Vin Fiz* first crossed the United States in 1911. The flight took more than 82 hours!

- Inventors created the first successful helicopter thirty years after the Wright brothers produced their biplane.

- In 1908, Madame Therese Peltier became the first woman to fly an airplane.

- Germans made the first jets in 1939.

- The Goodyear Tire company has flown a blimp to advertise its tires since 1925.

- Some historians say the name *blimp* comes from the sound the machine makes when you tap it with your finger.

Glossary

aircraft   a machine that flies

biplane   an airplane with two wings, one above the other, that stretch across the plane

blimp   a machine that flies with helium and air

commercial airplane   an airplane that carries large groups of people from place to place

corporate jet   a plane used by a business to fly its workers

fixed-wing a wing of an airplane that does not move

freight airplane an airplane that carries packages

helicopter a machine that flies using a large whirling blade on top

helium a gas that is used to fill balloons

hover to stay in one place in the air

military airplane an airplane equipped with weapons

Osprey an aircraft that is a combination of a helicopter and an airplane

seaplane a plane that takes off and lands on water

Shuttle Carrier Aircraft an airplane that carries the space shuttle on Earth

Index

Web Finder

http://www.wright-brothers.org/History/History of%20 Airplane/history.htm

http://science.howstuffworks.com/blimp1.htm

http://www.nasm.si.edu/